The hospital party

Story by Dawn McMillan

Illustrations by Brian Harrison

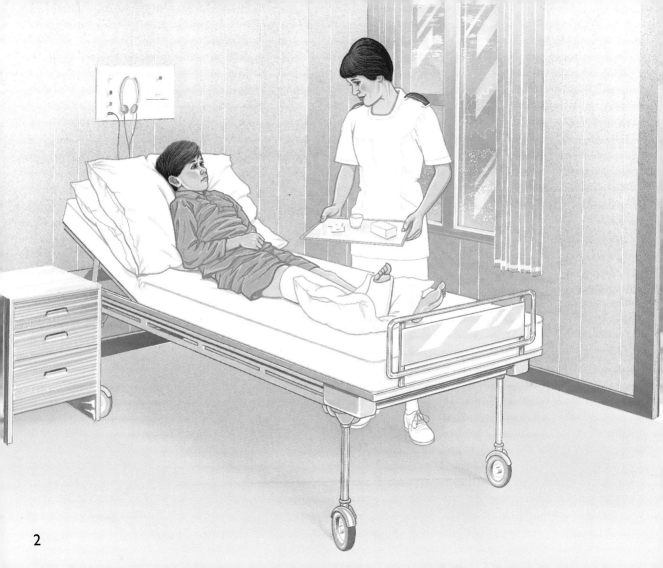

Adam had broken his leg.

He had to stay in the hospital

for two nights.

Adam said to the nurse,

"Tim is one of my best friends.

It is his birthday today,

and I can't go to his party."

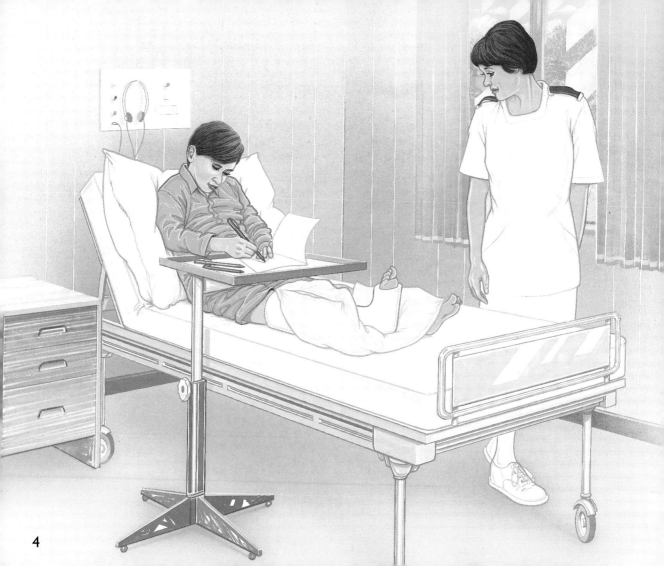

"Oh, dear," said the nurse.

"But you can make him

a birthday card.

I will get you some markers and paper."

Adam made a card for Tim.

Then Adam put the card

on the table by his bed.

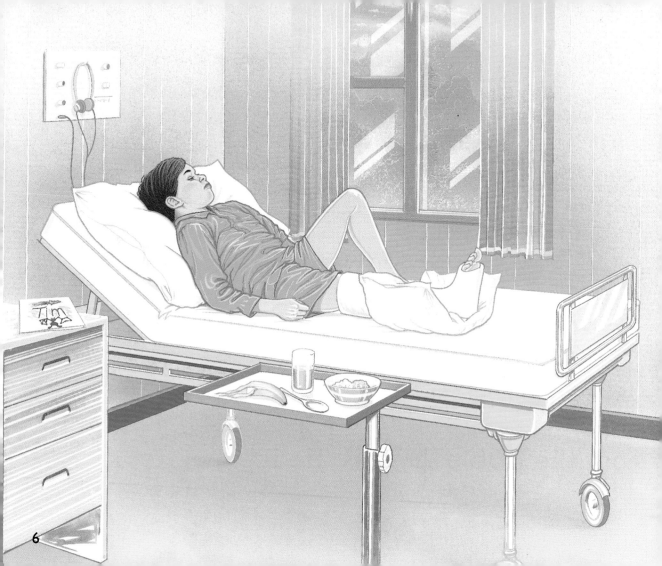

All that morning, Adam was sad.

He did not want to eat his lunch.

He looked out the window.

"I don't like it here in the hospital,"

he said to himself.

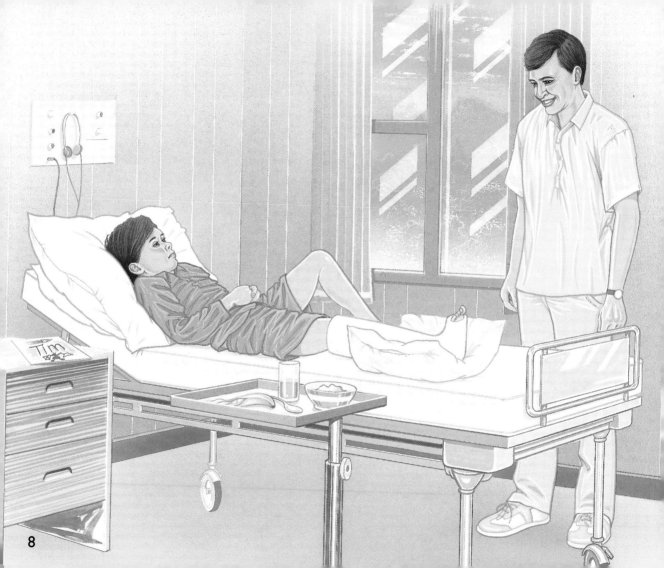

After lunch, Dad came in the door.
"Hello, Adam," he smiled.

Adam looked up,
but he was not smiling.
"I want to go home with you," he said,
"and I want to go to Tim's party."

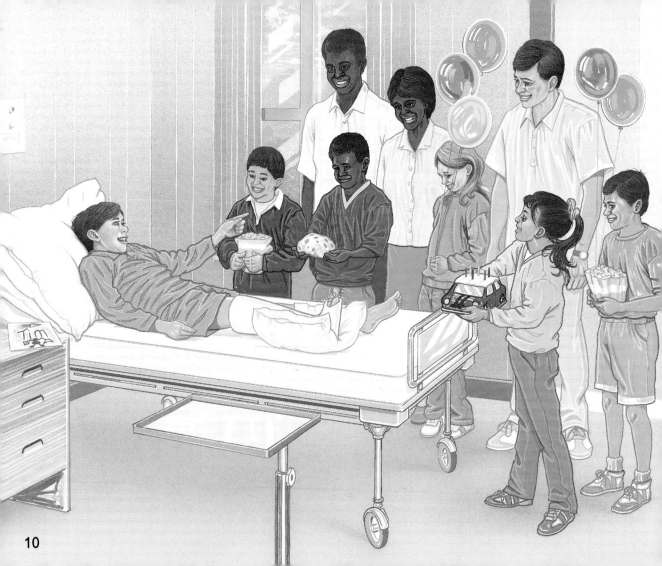

Then Tim came in the door,

with his mother and father.

Four of Tim's friends came with them.

The children had balloons, popcorn,

and Tim's birthday cake.

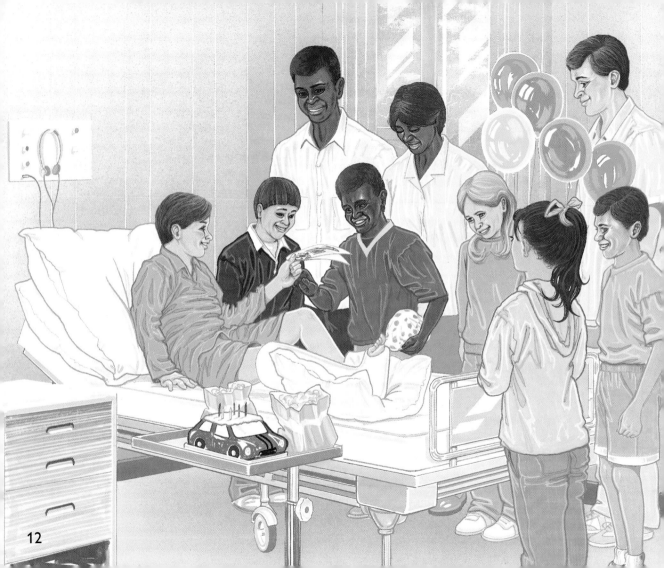

"Hi, Adam," said Tim.
"You can't come to my house,
so we are going to have
the party here."

"I made this card for you, Tim,"
said Adam. "Happy birthday."

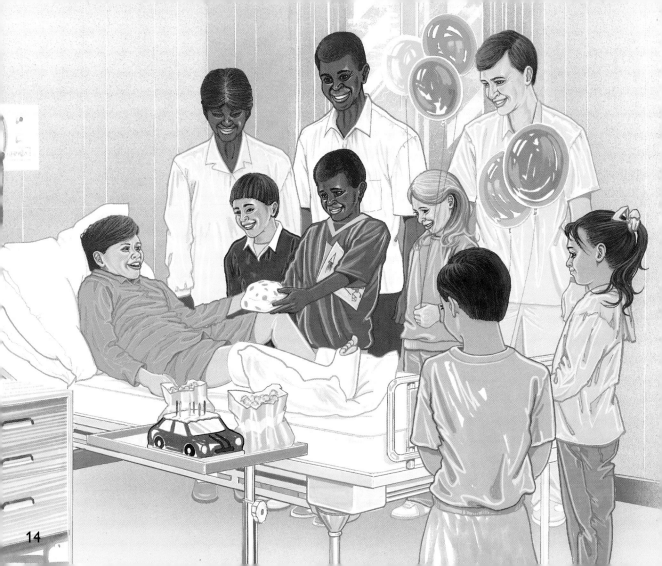

"Thanks, Adam," said Tim.

"I have a present for you."

"But it's not my birthday," said Adam.

"It's not a birthday present,"
laughed Tim.

"It's a hospital present!"

Adam smiled.

"I like hospital parties," he said.

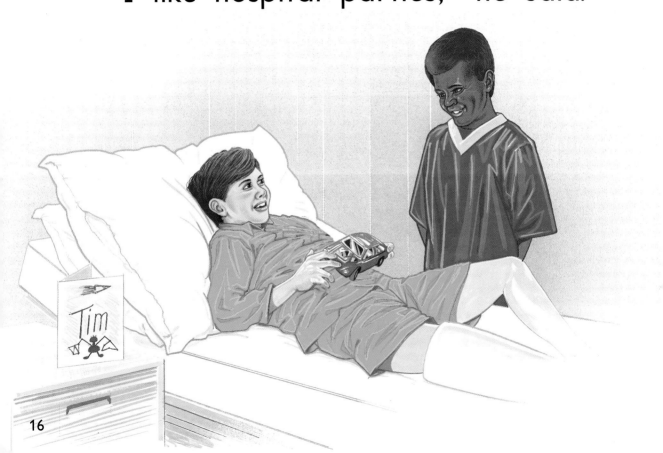